simply stir-fry

Chef
express

Published by:
TRIDENT REFERENCE PUBLISHING
801 12th Avenue South, Suite 400
Naples, Fl 34102 USA

Tel: + 1 (239) 649-7077
www.tridentreference.com
email: sales@tridentreference.com

simply
stir-fry

Simply Stir-Fry
© TRIDENT REFERENCE PUBLISHING

Publisher
Simon St. John Bailey

Editor-in-chief
Susan Knightley

Prepress
Precision Prep & Press

All rights reserved. No part of this book may
be stored, reproduced or transmitted in any
form and by any means without written
permission of the Publisher, except in the
case of brief quotations embodied in critical
articles and reviews.

Includes Index
ISBN 1582796769
UPC 6 15269 96769 0

Printed in The United States

introduction

Stir-frying entails simply frying foods in a small amount of oil over high heat, stirring constantly. This method, widely used in Oriental cookery, ensures that the food is sealed and cooked very quickly, which allows it to maintain its flavor, texture, and color —all so important to the success of the finished dish.

simply stir-fry
introduction

The key to stir-frying involves having the ingredients ready before you start cooking, which will take only minutes.
This is a healthy method, as stir-fried foods must not be overcooked or greasy.

The wok

- A wok, with its specially rounded base and sloping sides, is the perfect piece of equipment for stir-frying.

- Its shape allows the heat to spread evenly over the surface, which encourages rapid cooking, and its depth allows you to toss foods quickly.

- Choose a large wok with deep sides. The best ones are made of carbon steel, and must be seasoned before the first use.

- To season a wok, scrub it first to remove the machine oil which is applied by the manufacturer to protect it in transit, and

then dry it, and put it on the stovetop over a low heat. Add 2 tablespoons of cooking oil, and rub this all over the surface, using absorbent paper towels. Heat the wok slowly for 10-15 minutes and then wipe with more paper. Repeat the coating, heating, and wiping process until the paper comes away clean.

- You should never to scrub your wok again. Just wash in plain water and dry thoroughly by placing it over low heat for a few minutes before storing it. This will prevent your wok from rusting.

- Accessories you may find useful with your wok include a bamboo brush, which is used for cleaning the wok without scrubbing it.

Difficulty scale

■□□I Easy to do

■■□I Requires attention

■■■I Requires experience

tofu
in peanut sauce

■■□ I Cooking time: 15 minutes - Preparation time: 15 minutes

method

1. Cut tofu into large chunks and drain well. Heat oil in a wok over a high heat, add tofu and cook, turning several times, until golden. Drain on absorbent kitchen paper and set aside.

2. To make sauce, heat oil in a clean wok over a medium heat, add onion and stir-fry for 3 minutes or until golden. Add broccoli, zucchini and red pepper and stir-fry for 3 minutes. Add peanuts, soy sauce, plum sauce, miso and water and bring to simmering. Simmer, stirring occasionally, for 3 minutes.

3. Return tofu to wok and simmer for 2 minutes or until heated through.

....
Serves 4

ingredients

> **375 g/12 oz firm tofu**
> **vegetable oil for shallow-frying**

peanut sauce

> **2 teaspoons vegetable oil**
> **1 onion, chopped**
> **250 g/8 oz broccoli, broken into small flowerets**
> **2 zucchini, chopped**
> **1 red pepper, chopped**
> **75 g/2 1/2 oz peanuts, roasted and chopped**
> **1/4 cup/60 ml/2 fl oz soy sauce**
> **1/4 cup/60 ml/2 fl oz plum sauce**
> **2 teaspoons miso**
> **1/3 cup/90 ml/3 fl oz water**

tip from the chef

Tofu, also known as bean curd, is made from yellow soy beans which are soaked, ground and mixed with water then briefly cooked before being solidified. Rich in protein, it is low in fat and is cholesterol free. It is a good source of protein for those following a vegetarian diet.

red bean stir-fry

■□□ I Cooking time: 15 minutes - Preparation time: 15 minutes

ingredients

> 185 g/6 oz fettuccine
> 1 tablespoon vegetable oil
> 1 onion, chopped
> 2 cloves garlic, crushed
> 250 g/8 oz asparagus, cut into 5 cm/2 in lengths
> 125 g/4 oz green beans
> 125 g/4 oz snow peas
> 440 g/14 oz canned red kidney beans, rinsed and drained
> 250 g/8 oz bottled tomato salsa
> 2 tablespoons chopped fresh coriander
> 90 g/3 oz pine nuts, toasted

method

1. Cook fettuccine in boiling water in a large saucepan following packet directions. Drain well and set aside to cool slightly.
2. Heat oil in a wok over a medium heat, add onion and garlic and stir-fry for 3 minutes or until onion is golden.
3. Add asparagus, beans and snow peas and stir-fry for 3 minutes or until vegetables are just tender. Add red kidney beans, tomato salsa and coriander and stir-fry for 5 minutes.
4. Add fettuccine, toss to combine and cook for 3 minutes or until heated through. Scatter with pine nuts and serve immediately.

....
Serves 4

tip from the chef
Any pasta or Oriental noodles of your choice can be used in place of the fettuccine in this recipe.

tofu
and chinese greens

◼◼☐ | Cooking time: 12 minutes - Preparation time: 10 minutes

method

1. Place tofu, walnuts, ginger, coriander, soy sauce and sesame oil in a bowl and mix to combine. Cover and marinate at room temperature for 2 hours. Drain tofu and walnuts and reserve marinade.
2. Heat 1 tablespoon vegetable oil in a wok over a medium heat, add tofu and walnuts and stir-fry for 5 minutes or until tofu is golden. Remove from wok, set aside and keep warm.
3. Heat remaining vegetable oil in wok, add bok choy and broccoli and stir-fry for 3 minutes or until vegetables are just tender. Remove, place on a serving platter and keep warm.
4. Return tofu to wok, add reserved marinade and oyster and chili sauces and stir-fry for 3 minutes or until heated through. Place on top of vegetables. Serve immediately.

ingredients

> 315 g/10 oz firm tofu, cut into 2 cm/3/4 in cubes
> 60 g/2 oz walnuts, roughly chopped
> 1 tablespoon finely grated fresh ginger
> 1 tablespoon chopped fresh coriander
> 1/4 cup/60 ml/2 fl oz soy sauce
> 1 teaspoon sesame oil
> 2 tablespoons vegetable oil
> 1 bunch/500 g/1 lb bok choy, chopped
> 1 bunch/500 g/1 lb Chinese broccoli, chopped
> 1 tablespoon oyster sauce
> 1 tablespoon sweet chili sauce

Serves 4

tip from the chef

Chinese broccoli, also known as gai lum, resembles thin elongated Western broccoli with green stems and leaves and tiny white flowers. To use, trim base, remove tough stalks and cut into bite-sized pieces. The flowers are edible and should be included.

pad thai noodles

■■□ | Cooking time: 6 minutes - Preparation time: 15 minutes

method

1. Place eggs and soy and chili sauces in a bowl and whisk to combine. Set aside.
2. Heat oil in a wok over a medium heat, add spring onions, garlic and lemon grass and stir-fry for 2 minutes. Add noodles, broccoli, beans and red pepper and gently stir-fry for 3 minutes.
3. Add basil and toss to combine. Pour egg mixture into wok and cook, stirring, for 1 minute or until egg just sets. Serve immediately.

Serves 4

ingredients

> 2 eggs, lightly beaten
> 2 tablespoons soy sauce
> 2 tablespoons sweet chili sauce
> 2 teaspoons sesame oil
> 4 spring onions, chopped
> 1 clove garlic, crushed
> 1 stalk fresh lemon grass, chopped, or 1/2 teaspoon dried lemon grass, soaked
> 500 g/1 lb fresh rice noodles
> 125 g/4 oz broccoli, chopped
> 125 g/4 oz green beans, trimmed and chopped
> 1 red pepper, chopped
> 2 tablespoons chopped fresh basil

tip from the chef

Lemon grass is an aromatic herb, native of India. It is widely used in Thai and Vietnamese cooking.

bamboo
and noodles

■☐☐ I Cooking time: 12 minutes - Preparation time: 15 minutes

method

1. Cook noodles in boiling water in a large saucepan for 3 minutes or until tender. Drain, rinse under cold water, drain again and set aside.

2. Heat oil in a wok over a medium heat, add garlic, ginger and chilies and stir-fry for 2 minutes or until golden. Add bok choy, bamboo shoots, red pepper, spring onions and noodles and stir-fry for 3 minutes.

3. Add mushrooms and bean sprouts, then stir in soy, hoisin, oyster and chili sauces and stir-fry for 4 minutes or until heated through.

....

Serves 4

ingredients

- > **500 g/1 lb fresh hokkien noodles**
- > **2 teaspoons vegetable oil**
- > **2 cloves garlic, crushed**
- > **2 teaspoons finely grated fresh ginger**
- > **2 fresh red chilies, chopped**
- > **1 bunch/500 g/1 lb bok choy, chopped**
- > **220 g/7 oz canned bamboo shoots, drained and sliced**
- > **1 red pepper, chopped**
- > **6 spring onions, chopped**
- > **155 g/5 oz oyster mushrooms**
- > **60 g/2 oz bean sprouts**
- > **1^1/2 tablespoons soy sauce**
- > **1^1/2 tablespoons hoisin sauce**
- > **1 tablespoon oyster sauce**
- > **1 tablespoon sweet chili sauce**

tip from the chef

Hokkien noodles are Chinese egg noodles, they are available from Oriental food stores and range from wide ribbon noodles to thin spaghetti-style noodles. Any ribbon pasta such linguine, fettuccine or spaghetti can be used in their place.

indian
yogurt fish

■■□ | Cooking time: 20 minutes - Preparation time: 20 minutes

ingredients
> 1 tablespoon vegetable oil
> 1 onion, finely chopped
> 1 tablespoon black
  mustard seeds
> 1 tablespoon ground
  coriander
> 1 teaspoon ground cumin
> 1 teaspoon ground
  turmeric
> 1 tablespoon tandoori
  curry paste
> 500 g/1 lb firm white fish
  fillets, cut into 2 cm/
  $3/4$ in cubes
> 2 tablespoons chopped
  fresh mint
> 1 tablespoon chopped
  fresh coriander
> 1 cup/250 ml/8 fl oz
  tomato purée
> $1/2$ cup/100 g/$3^1/2$ oz
  natural yogurt
> 2 teaspoons sesame oil
> 2 cloves garlic, crushed
> 1 bunch/500 g/1 lb bok
  choy, chopped
> 2 tablespoons shredded
  coconut, toasted

method
1. Heat vegetable oil in a wok over a medium heat, add onion, mustard seeds, coriander, cumin, turmeric and curry paste and stir-fry for 3 minutes or until onion is tender. Add fish, stir-fry for 5 minutes (a) or until fish is almost cooked.
2. Stir in mint, coriander and tomato purée and simmer for 5 minutes or until heated through. Reduce heat, stir in yogurt and cook (b), without boiling, for 2 minutes longer. Remove fish mixture from wok, set aside and keep warm.
3. Heat sesame oil in a clean wok over a medium heat, add garlic and stir-fry for 2 minutes or until golden. Increase heat to high, add bok choy and coconut (c) and stir-fry for 3 minutes or until bok choy is tender.
4. Divide bok choy mixture between serving plates, top with fish mixture.

....
Serves 4

tip from the chef
It is important the fish mixture not to boil after the yogurt has been added, or it will curdle.

a

b

c

fish with rice noodles

■□□ | Cooking time: 10 minutes - Preparation time: 10 minutes

method

1. Heat sesame and vegetable oils together in a wok over a medium heat, add lemon grass and stir-fry for 1 minute. Add fish, coriander and lime juice and stir-fry for 1 minute or until fish is golden. Remove fish mixture from wok and set aside.

2. Add asparagus, broccoli and chili and soy sauces to wok and stir-fry for 2 minutes. Add noodles and gently stir-fry for 2 minutes longer, then return fish mixture to pan and cook for 1 minute or until heated through. Serve immediately.

....

Serves 4

ingredients

> 1 teaspoon sesame oil
> 1 teaspoon vegetable oil
> 1 stalk fresh lemon grass, chopped, or 1/2 teaspoon dried lemon grass, soaked
> 500 g/1 lb ocean trout or salmon fillets, cut into 2 cm/3/4 in thick strips
> 2 tablespoons chopped fresh coriander
> 2 tablespoons lime juice
> 250 g/8 oz asparagus, chopped
> 185 g/6 oz broccoli, chopped
> 3 tablespoons sweet chili sauce
> 2 tablespoons soy sauce
> 500 g/1 lb fresh rice noodles

tip from the chef

Fresh rice noodles are lightly cooked soft, wet noodles made from a sweet glutinous rice. They are available in plastic packages in the refrigerator section of Oriental food stores. Take care when cooking the noodles as they are delicate and can easily be overcooked.

lemon
grass tuna

■□□ I Cooking time: 15 minutes - Preparation time: 15 minutes

ingredients

> 250 g/8 oz fresh egg
  noodles
> 1 tablespoon peanut oil
> 1 teaspoon sesame oil
> 1 onion, cut into eighths
> 1 tablespoon finely grated
  fresh ginger
> 2 stalks fresh lemon
  grass, chopped,
  or 1 teaspoon dried lemon
  grass, soaked
> 1 small fresh red chili,
  finely chopped
> 3 tuna steaks, cut into
  thick strips
> 250 g/8 oz asparagus, cut
  into 5 cm/2 in lengths
> 1 red pepper, chopped
> 125 g/4 oz snow peas
> freshly ground black
  pepper
> 2 tablespoons flaked
  almonds, toasted

basil and coconut sauce

> 2 tablespoons chopped
  fresh basil
> 1/2 cup/125 ml/4 fl oz
  coconut milk
> 1 tablespoon each fish
  and sweet chili sauces
> 1 tablespoon lime juice

method

1. Cook noodles in boiling water in a saucepan
   following packet directions. Drain, set aside
   and keep warm.
2. To make sauce, place basil, coconut milk,
   fish and chili sauces and lime juice in
   a bowl and mix to combine. Set aside.
3. Heat peanut and sesame oils together
   in a wok over a medium heat, add onion,
   ginger, lemon grass and chili and stir-fry
   for 3 minutes or until onion is golden.
   Add tuna and stir-fry for 3 minutes or until
   it just changes color. Remove mixture from
   wok, set aside and keep warm.
4. Add asparagus, red pepper and snow peas
   to wok and stir-fry for 3 minutes or until
   vegetables are just tender. Return tuna
   mixture to wok, stir in sauce and bring
   to the boil. Reduce heat and simmer
   for 3 minutes or until sauce thickens
   slightly. Season to taste with black pepper.
5. Divide noodles between serving plates, top
   with tuna mixture and scatter with
   almonds.

....
Serves 4

tip from the chef

*Fresh lemon grass is available from Oriental
food shops and some supermarkets and
greengrocers. It is also available dried; if
using dried lemon grass soak it in hot water
for 20 minutes or until soft before using.*

lime fish

■ ■ □ | Cooking time: 8 minutes - Preparation time: 10 minutes

method

1. Heat oil in a wok over a high heat, add spring onions, lemon grass and chili and stir-fry for 1 minute. Add fish and lime juice and stir-fry (a) for 2 minutes or until fish is almost cooked. Remove fish mixture from wok and set aside.

2. Add noodles, bok choy, water, soy sauce and miso to wok and stir-fry for 2 minutes. Return fish mixture to wok (b) and stir-fry for 1 minute or until heated through.

Serves 4

ingredients

> 2 teaspoons vegetable oil
> 3 spring onions, chopped
> 1 stalk fresh lemon grass, chopped, or 1/2 teaspoon dried lemon grass, soaked
> 1 fresh red chili, chopped
> 750 g/1 1/2 lb firm white fish fillets, cut into 2 cm/3/4 in thick strips
> 2 tablespoons lime juice
> 315 g/10 oz fresh rice noodles
> 1/2 bunch/250 g/8 oz bok choy, chopped
> 1/4 cup/60 ml/2 fl oz water
> 2 tablespoons soy sauce
> 2 teaspoons white miso

a

b

tip from the chef

Serve this easy and healthy one-dish meal with lime wedges. Ordinary cabbage, spinach or silverbeet can be used in place of bok choy.

seafood
and oyster mushrooms

■■□ I Cooking time: 5 minutes - Preparation time: 5 minutes

ingredients

> 8 uncooked medium prawns, shelled and deveined
> 125 g/4 oz squid tubes, honeycombed
> 8 baby octopus, cleaned
> 155 g/5 oz scallops
> 2 teaspoons vegetable oil
> 250 g/8 oz oyster mushrooms
> 6 spring onions, chopped
> freshly ground black pepper

chili coriander marinade

> 3 tablespoons chopped fresh coriander
> 2 cloves garlic, crushed
> 4 tablespoons Worcestershire sauce
> 1/3 cup/90 ml/3 fl oz soy sauce
> 2 tablespoons sweet chili sauce

method

1. To make marinade, place coriander, garlic and Worcestershire, soy and chili sauces in a bowl and mix to combine. Add prawns, squid, octopus and scallops and toss to combine. Cover and marinate in the refrigerator for 2-3 hours.

2. Drain seafood and reserve marinade. Heat oil in a wok over a high heat, add seafood and stir-fry for 2 minutes. Add mushrooms, spring onions and 3 tablespoons reserved marinade and stir-fry for 2 minutes longer or until seafood is cooked. Season to taste with black pepper.

....

Serves 4

tip from the chef

To honeycomb squid, make a single cut down the length of the tube and open out flat with inside facing up. Using a sharp knife, cut parallel lines down the length of the squid, taking care not to cut right through the flesh. Then make more cuts in the opposite direction to form a diamond pattern.

seafood
stir-fry

■■□ | Cooking time: 6 minutes - Preparation time: 20 minutes

method

1. Heat peanut oil in a wok or frying pan, add garlic, chilies and ginger and stir-fry for 1 minute. Add squid, prawns, scallops, red pepper, snow peas and asparagus and stir-fry for 2-3 minutes or until prawns just change color.

2. To make sauce, place cornflour, sugar, tomato, oyster and soy sauces, sesame oil and water in a small bowl and whisk to combine. Pour sauce into pan and heat for 2-3 minutes longer or until it boils and thickens. Sprinkle with sesame seeds and serve immediately.

....
Serves 4

ingredients

> 2 tablespoons peanut oil
> 1 clove garlic, crushed
> 2 small fresh red chilies, finely chopped
> 1 teaspoon finely grated fresh ginger
> 250 g/8 oz squid tubes, honeycombed (see tip page 24) and cut into diamond-shaped pieces
> 500 g/1 lb uncooked large prawns, shelled and deveined, tails left intact
> 250 g/8 oz scallops
> 1/2 red pepper, sliced
> 60 g/2 oz snow peas, sliced diagonally into 5 cm/2 in pieces
> 250 g/8 oz asparagus, cut diagonally into 5 cm/2 in pieces, blanched
> 2 tablespoons sesame seeds, toasted

sauce

> 1 tablespoon cornflour
> 1 tablespoon sugar
> 3 tablespoons bottled tomato sauce
> 1 teaspoon oyster sauce
> 1 tablespoon soy sauce
> 1 teaspoon sesame oil
> 1 cup/250 ml/8 fl oz water

tip from the chef

For a complete meal accompany with boiled egg noodles.

chicken
and pepper salad

■■□ | Cooking time: 7 minutes - Preparation time: 10 minutes

method

1. Heat sesame and chili oils together in a wok over a medium heat, add lemon grass and stir-fry for 2 minutes or until golden.
2. Add chicken, water chestnuts and soy sauce and stir-fry for 5 minutes or until chicken is tender. Transfer to a bowl and cool slightly.
3. Add red pepper, green pepper, bean sprouts and coconut and toss to combine. Arrange mixture on a large platter, over lettuce leaves.
4. To make dressing, place mint, garlic, sugar, water, fish sauce and lime juice in a bowl and mix to combine. Spoon over salad and serve.

Serves 4

ingredients

> 1 teaspoon sesame oil
> 1 teaspoon chili oil
> 1 stalk fresh lemon grass, chopped, or $1/2$ teaspoon dried lemon grass, soaked
> 315 g/10 oz lean chicken mince
> 185 g/6 oz water chestnuts, chopped
> 1 tablespoon soy sauce
> 1 each red and green pepper, thinly sliced
> 60 g/2 oz bean sprouts
> $1/2$ cup/45 g/$1 1/2$ oz shredded coconut, toasted
> assorted lettuce leaves

mint dressing

> 3 tablespoons chopped fresh mint
> 1 clove garlic, crushed
> 1 tablespoon brown sugar
> $1/4$ cup/60 ml/2 fl oz water
> 1 tablespoon fish sauce
> 1 tablespoon lime juice

tip from the chef

Fish sauce is a pungent Oriental ingredient that is extensively used in Thai cooking. It is available from Oriental food shops and some supermarkets.

tomato
pesto chicken

■ □ □ | Cooking time: 15 minutes - Preparation time: 15 minutes

ingredients

> 1 tablespoon olive oil
> 1 onion, cut into eighths
> 4 boneless chicken breast fillets, each cut into 3 pieces
> 1 cup/250 ml/8 fl oz tomato purée
> freshly ground black pepper

tomato pesto

> 1 bunch fresh basil
> 125 g/4 oz sun-dried tomatoes
> 4 tablespoons grated fresh Parmesan cheese
> 2 cloves garlic, chopped
> 2 tablespoons pine nuts
> 1/2 cup/125 ml/4 fl oz olive oil

method

1. To make pesto, place basil leaves, sun-dried tomatoes, Parmesan cheese, garlic and pine nuts in a food processor (a) and process until smooth. With machine running, gradually add 1/2 cup/125 ml/4 fl oz oil and process until mixture forms a smooth paste.

2. Heat remaining oil in a wok over a high heat, add onion and stir-fry for 2 minutes. Add chicken and stir-fry for 5 minutes or until tender (b). Add tomato purée and stir-fry for 5 minutes or until heated through. Season to taste with black pepper (c). Serve with pesto.

....

Serves 4

tip from the chef

For a complete meal serve with boiled pasta of your choice or crusty bread and a tossed salad of mixed lettuce leaves.

a

b

c

curry chicken with greens

■□□ | Cooking time: 15 minutes - Preparation time: 10 minutes

method

1. Heat half the oil in a wok over a medium heat, add cashews and stir-fry for 4 minutes or until golden. Remove from wok and set aside.
2. Heat remaining oil in wok over a high heat, add chicken and lemon grass and stir-fry for 4 minutes or until chicken is brown.
3. Add chili, sugar, curry paste, lime juice and fish and oyster sauces. Return cashews to wok and stir-fry for 5 minutes.
4. Arrange bok choy on a serving platter and top with chicken mixture.

....
Serves 4

ingredients

- > 1 tablespoon vegetable oil
- > 90 g/3 oz raw cashews
- > 4 boneless chicken breast fillets, sliced
- > 1 stalk fresh lemon grass, chopped, or 1/2 teaspoon dried lemon grass, soaked
- > 1 fresh red chili, chopped
- > 2 tablespoons brown sugar
- > 2 teaspoons curry paste
- > 1/4 cup/60 ml/2 fl oz lime juice
- > 2 tablespoons fish sauce
- > 2 tablespoons oyster sauce
- > 1 bunch/500 g/1 lb bok choy, steamed

tip from the chef

Oyster sauce is a staple Oriental ingredient made from a concentrate of oysters cooked in soy sauce and brine. It is dark brown in color and has a rich flavor.

spiced
coconut chicken

■■□ | Cooking time: 10 minutes - Preparation time: 10 minutes

ingredients

> **2 teaspoons vegetable oil**
> **2 stalks fresh lemon grass, chopped or 1 teaspoon dried lemon grass, soaked**
> **2 teaspoons finely grated fresh ginger**
> **1 teaspoon ground cumin**
> **4 boneless chicken breast fillets, cut into thick slices**
> **3 tablespoons chopped fresh coriander**
> **1 cup/250 ml/8 fl oz coconut milk**
> **1/2 cup/125 ml/4 fl oz chicken stock**
> **125 g/4 oz snow peas, trimmed**
> **freshly ground black pepper**
> **4 tablespoons peanuts, roasted and chopped**

method

1. Heat oil in a wok over a high heat, add lemon grass, ginger and cumin and stir-fry for 1 minute. Add chicken and stir-fry for 3 minutes or until golden.
2. Stir in coriander, coconut milk and stock, bring to simmering and simmer for 5 minutes. Add snow peas and cook for 1 minute or until they change color. Season to taste with black pepper. Scatter with peanuts and serve.

....
Serves 4

tip from the chef

For a complete meal serve on a bed of fragrant rice. Jasmine or basmati rice are both readily available from supermarkets and Oriental food stores.

garlic
pepper chicken

■■□ | Cooking time: 10 minutes - Preparation time: 10 minutes

method

1. Heat oil in a wok over a medium heat, add garlic and black peppercorns and stir-fry for 1 minute or until garlic is golden.
Add chicken and stir-fry for 3 minutes or until brown.

2. Stir in stock, wine and soy sauce, bring to simmering and simmer for 4 minutes or until sauce reduces by half.

3. Arrange spinach leaves on serving plates and top with chicken mixture. Serve immediately.

Serves 4

ingredients

> **2 teaspoons vegetable oil**
> **4 cloves garlic, crushed**
> **1 teaspoon crushed black peppercorns**
> **4 boneless chicken breast fillets, sliced**
> **1/2 cup/125 ml/4 fl oz chicken stock**
> **1/4 cup/60 ml/2 fl oz dry white wine**
> **1 tablespoon soy sauce**
> **155 g/5 oz young English spinach leaves**

tip from the chef

When buying a wok, choose a large one –with at least a 35 cm/14 in diameter and deep sides. A heavy wok made of carbon steel is better than a light stainless steel or aluminum one. Remember it is easier to cook a small amount of food in a large wok than to cook a large amount of food in a small wok!

creamy chicken and mushrooms

■■□ | Cooking time: 25 minutes - Preparation time: 10 minutes

ingredients

> 1 tablespoon walnut oil
> 2 cloves garlic, crushed
> 2 rashers bacon, chopped
> 4 boneless chicken breast fillets, sliced
> 4 spring onions, chopped
> 375 g/12 oz mixed mushrooms
> 3 large field mushrooms
> 1/4 cup/60 ml/2 fl oz brandy
> 1 cup/250 ml/8 fl oz cream
> 1/2 cup/125 ml/4 fl oz chicken stock
> freshly ground black pepper

method

1. Heat oil in wok over a medium heat, add garlic and bacon and stir-fry for 3 minutes or until brown. Add chicken and stir-fry for 5 minutes or until tender. Remove chicken mixture from wok, set aside and keep warm.

2. Add spring onions and mixed and field mushrooms to wok and stir-fry for 2 minutes or until tender. Return chicken mixture to wok, stir in brandy, cream and stock and bring to boil. Reduce heat and simmer for 15 minutes or until sauce reduces by half. Season to taste with black pepper.

Serves 4

tip from the chef

Most larger supermarkets and greengrocers sell a range of mushrooms –look out for varieties such as shiitake, oyster and enoki. If you can only find ordinary mushrooms, add a few dried ones for extra flavor –remember to soak them in warm water before using.

provençal chicken

■ ■ □ | Cooking time: 25 minutes - Preparation time: 5 minutes

method

1. Heat oil in a wok over a medium heat, add onion, garlic and capers and stir-fry for 3 minutes or until onion is golden.
2. Add chicken and stir-fry for 5 minutes or until chicken is brown. Add beans, artichokes and olives and stir-fry for 3 minutes longer.
3. Stir in tomato sauce and parsley and cook, stirring frequently, for 10 minutes or until sauce thickens slightly. Season to taste with black pepper.

Serves 4

ingredients

> 1 tablespoon vegetable oil
> 1 red onion, chopped
> 2 cloves garlic, crushed
> 2 tablespoons capers, drained and chopped
> 4 boneless chicken thighs, chopped
> 440 g/14 oz canned cannellini beans, rinsed and drained
> 200 g/6^1/2 oz marinated artichoke hearts
> 125 g/4 oz kalamata olives, pitted
> 1^1/2 cups/375 ml/ 12 fl oz bottled tomato sauce
> 2 tablespoons chopped fresh parsley
> freshly ground black pepper

tip from the chef

Dried cannellini beans can be used instead of canned, however you will need to soak and cook them before using. To prepare and cook dried beans, soak beans overnight in cold water. Drain beans and place in a large saucepan. Cover with fresh cold water, bring to the boil and boil for 10 minutes. Reduce heat and simmer for 1-1^1/2 hours or until beans are tender. Drain well and use as desired.

honey beef
with salsa

■□□ | Cooking time: 10 minutes - Preparation time: 15 minutes

method

1. Heat oil in a wok over a medium heat, add sesame seeds and garlic and stir-fry for 2 minutes or until seeds are golden. Remove seed mixture from wok and set aside.
2. Add beef to wok and stir-fry for 2 minutes or until brown (a). Add snow peas, zucchini, honey and soy and oyster sauces. Return sesame seed mixture to wok (b) and stir-fry for 3 minutes or until sauce thickens.
3. To make salsa, place pineapple, chili, sugar, chives and lime juice in a bowl and toss to combine (c). Serve with beef.

....
Serves 4

ingredients

> **2 teaspoons vegetable oil**
> **2 tablespoons sesame seeds**
> **2 cloves garlic, crushed**
> **500 g/1 lb lean beef strips**
> **185 g/6 oz snow peas, trimmed**
> **2 zucchini, chopped**
> **3 tablespoons honey**
> **2 tablespoons soy sauce**
> **1 tablespoon oyster sauce**

pineapple salsa

> **1/2 fresh pineapple, peeled, cored and chopped**
> **1 fresh red chili, chopped**
> **2 tablespoons brown sugar**
> **2 tablespoons snipped fresh chives**
> **2 tablespoons lime juice**

tip from the chef

When handling fresh chilies do not put your hands near your eyes or allow them to touch your lips. To avoid discomfort and burning wear rubber gloves.

a

b

c

beef
and broccoli curry

■ ■ □ | Cooking time: 20 minutes - Preparation time: 10 minutes

method

1. Heat oil in a wok over a medium heat, add onion, garlic and ginger and stir-fry for 3 minutes or until golden. Add curry paste and stir-fry for 2 minutes or until fragrant. Increase heat to high, add beef and stir-fry for 5 minutes or until brown.

2. Add broccoli and red pepper and stir-fry for 3 minutes or until just tender. Stir in sugar, lime rind, coconut milk and fish sauce and simmer for 5 minutes or until sauce is heated. Scatter with peanuts and serve.

....
Serves 4

ingredients

> 1 tablespoon peanut oil
> 1 onion, chopped
> 2 cloves garlic, crushed
> 1 tablespoon finely grated fresh ginger
> 1 tablespoon red curry paste
> 500 g/1 lb rump steak, trimmed of all visible fat, cut into thin strips
> 250 g/8 oz broccoli, cut into small pieces
> 1 red pepper, chopped
> 1 tablespoon brown sugar
> 1 teaspoon finely grated lime rind
> 1 1/2 cups/375 ml/ 12 fl oz coconut milk
> 1 tablespoon fish sauce
> 155 g/5 oz peanuts, roasted

tip from the chef

To roast peanuts, spread nuts out evenly on a baking tray and bake at 180°C/350°F/Gas 4 for 5-10 minutes or until lightly and evenly browned. Toss back and forth occasionally with a spoon to ensure even browning. Alternatively, roast nuts under a preheated medium grill.

beef
and vegetable stir-fry

■■■ | Cooking time: 30 minutes - Preparation time: 15 minutes

method

1. To make mayonnaise, place egg yolk, lemon juice and mustard in food processor or blender and process to combine. With machine running, gradually add oil and process until thick. Place mayonnaise in a bowl, stir in coriander and black pepper to taste. Cover and refrigerate until required.

2. Place eggplant into a colander, sprinkle with salt and drain for 30 minutes. Rinse under running water and dry on absorbent kitchen paper.

3. Combine garlic, thyme and olive oil. Brush eggplant with oil mixture, place on a baking tray and bake at 180°C/350°F/Gas 4 for 20 minutes or until tender.

4. Heat vegetable oil in a wok over a high heat, add beef and stir-fry for 4 minutes or until brown. Add yellow or red pepper, sun-dried tomatoes and eggplant and stir-fry for 3 minutes or until pepper is tender. Season to taste with black pepper. Serve with mayonnaise.

....
Serves 4

ingredients

> **6 baby eggplant, halved lengthwise**
> **sea salt**
> **3 cloves garlic, crushed**
> **1 tablespoon chopped fresh thyme**
> **2 tablespoons olive oil**
> **2 teaspoons vegetable oil**
> **500 g/1 lb rump steak, trimmed of all visible fat, cut into thin strips**
> **1 yellow or red pepper, sliced**
> **4 tablespoons chopped sun-dried tomatoes**

coriander mayonnaise

> **1 egg yolk**
> **1 tablespoon lemon juice**
> **1/2 teaspoon Dijon mustard**
> **155 ml/5 fl oz olive oil**
> **3 tablespoons finely chopped coriander**
> **freshly ground black pepper**

tip from the chef

All this tasty dish needs to make a complete meal is boiled rice or pasta of your choice.

veal with
sun-dried tomatoes

■□□ I Cooking time: 15 minutes - Preparation time: 15 minutes

method

1. Heat reserved sun-dried tomato oil in a wok over moderate heat. Add veal, cook for 1 minute, remove with a slotted spoon and set aside.
2. Add olive oil to wok, heat, then add onion, garlic, tomato, squash, rosemary and tomato paste, cook for 2 minutes.
3. Combine stock, wine and flour and add to wok, cook until reduced by half, about 10 minutes.
4. Stir in veal, sun-dried tomatoes and parsley. Serve immediately.

....
Serves 4

ingredients

- > 1/2 cup marinated sun-dried tomatoes, reserve 4 tablespoons of oil
- > 500 g/1 lb veal fillets, cut into strips
- > 2 tablespoons olive oil
- > 1 red onion, chopped
- > 2 cloves garlic, crushed
- > 1 tomato, finely chopped
- > 200 g/6 1/2 oz baby squash, quartered
- > 1 tablespoon finely chopped fresh rosemary
- > 2 tablespoons tomato paste (purée)
- > 1/2 cup chicken stock
- > 1/4 cup dry white wine
- > 1 teaspoon plain flour
- > 1 tablespoon finely chopped parsley

tip from the chef

For variation, baby eggplant can be used in place of baby squash.

marinated
lamb with spinach

■■□I Cooking time: 15 minutes - Preparation time: 15 minutes

ingredients

> 3 cloves garlic, crushed
> 2 tablespoons chopped fresh oregano
> 2 tablespoons wholegrain mustard
> 1/2 cup/125 ml/4 fl oz red wine
> 2 tablespoons Worcestershire sauce
> 2 tablespoons honey
> 500 g/1 lb lamb fillet, trimmed of all visible fat, cut into thin slices
> 2 potatoes, peeled and cut into 3 mm/1/8 in thick matchsticks
> 2 tablespoons vegetable oil
> 1 bunch/500 g/1 lb English spinach, stems removed
> 155 g/5 oz button mushrooms, sliced
> freshly ground black pepper

method

1. Place garlic, oregano, mustard, wine, Worcestershire sauce and honey in a bowl and mix to combine. Add lamb, toss to coat with marinade, cover and refrigerate for at least 4 hours.

2. Place potatoes in a bowl, cover with cold water and soak for 1 hour. Drain potatoes, rinse under cold running water and dry on absorbent kitchen paper.

3. Heat oil in a wok over a medium heat, add potatoes and stir-fry for 6 minutes or until golden and tender. Remove potatoes from wok, set aside and keep warm.

4. Drain lamb and reserve marinade. Add lamb to wok and stir-fry for 4 minutes or until brown. Add spinach, mushrooms and reserved marinade and stir-fry for 4 minutes or until spinach wilts. Season to taste with black pepper. To serve, divide potatoes between serving plates, then top with lamb mixture.

....
Serves 4

tip from the chef
Always drain marinated food well before cooking. Wet food will stew rather than brown.

caramelized
onions and lamb

method

1. Heat butter and vegetable oil together in a wok over a medium heat, add onions, sugar and red wine vinegar and stir-fry for 10 minutes or until onions are caramelized.
2. Add cabbage and beans and stir-fry for 5 minutes or until cabbage wilts. Remove vegetable mixture from wok, set aside and keep warm.
3. Heat chili oil in wok over a high heat, add lamb and cook for 3 minutes each side or until cooked to your liking. Remove from wok, set aside and keep warm. Add rice wine, kechap manis and balsamic vinegar to wok and simmer for 5 minutes or until sauce thickens slightly.
4. To serve, cut lamb into thin slices. Divide vegetable mixture between serving plates, top with lamb slices and spoon over sauce.

Serves 4

ingredients

> 30 g/1 oz butter
> 1 tablespoon vegetable oil
> 2 onions, thinly sliced
> 1 tablespoon brown sugar
> 1 tablespoon red wine vinegar
> 1/4 red cabbage, shredded
> 100 g/3 1/2 oz green beans, trimmed
> 1 tablespoon chili oil
> 500 g/1 lb lamb fillet, trimmed of all visible fat
> 1/4 cup/60 ml/2 fl oz rice wine
> 1/4 cup/60 ml/2 fl oz kechap manis
> 1 tablespoon balsamic vinegar

tip from the chef

Kechap manis is a thick sweet seasoning sauce, made of soy sauce, sugar and spices. If unavailable a mixture of soy sauce and golden syrup can be used in its place.

lamb stir-fry

■■□ | Cooking time: 20 minutes - Preparation time: 15 minutes

ingredients

> **2 tablespoons sesame oil**
> **500 g/1 lb lamb fillet, trimmed of all visible fat, cut into thin strips**
> **1 onion, cut into wedges and layers separated**
> **1 tablespoon finely grated fresh ginger**
> **1 clove garlic, crushed**
> **1 red pepper, seeded and cut into thin strips**
> **1 carrot, sliced diagonally**
> **250 g/8 oz broccoli flowerets**
> **125 g/4 oz snow peas, trimmed**
> **2 tablespoons soy sauce**
> **1 tablespoon oyster sauce**
> **1 tablespoon honey**
> **2 teaspoons cornflour blended with
> 1 tablespoon water**

method

1. Heat sesame oil in a wok over a high heat. Add half the lamb and stir-fry for 5 minutes or until brown (a). Remove lamb from wok and set aside. Repeat with remaining lamb.
2. Add onion, ginger and garlic to wok and stir-fry for 2 minutes. Add red pepper, carrot, broccoli and snow peas (b) and stir-fry for 5 minutes or until vegetables change color and are just tender.
3. Return meat to wok, stir in soy sauce, oyster sauce and honey (c) and stir-fry for 1 minute. Stir in cornflour mixture and stir-fry for 1-2 minutes longer or until sauce boils and thickens slightly. Serve immediately.

Serves 4

tip from the chef

Sesame oil is a strongly flavored oil made from roasted sesame seeds. It is available from Oriental food stores and some supermarkets and keeps indefinitely.

a

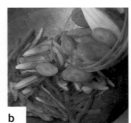

b

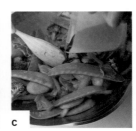

c

country lamb

■ ■ □ | Cooking time: 15 minutes - Preparation time: 15 minutes

method

1. To make sauce, combine stock, wine, passata and Worcestershire sauce in a bowl. Set aside.
2. Heat oil in a wok over a medium heat, add onion and garlic and stir-fry for 3 minutes or until golden.
3. Increase heat to high, add lamb and stir-fry for 5 minutes or until brown. Remove lamb from wok, set aside and keep warm.
4. Add carrot, zucchini, sugar snap peas or snow peas and mushrooms to wok and stir-fry for 5 minutes or until vegetables are tender.
5. Return lamb to wok, stir in sauce and cornflour mixture, bring to the boil and cook, stirring, for 1-2 minutes or until sauce thickens slightly. Stir in parsley and season with black pepper.

....
Serves 4

ingredients

> 1 tablespoon vegetable oil
> 1 onion, chopped
> 1 clove garlic, crushed
> 500 g/1 lb lean lamb, cut into strips
> 1 carrot, sliced
> 2 zucchini, sliced
> 125 g/4 oz sugar snap peas or snow peas
> 125 g/4 oz button mushrooms
> 1 tablespoon cornflour blended with 1 tablespoon water
> 2 tablespoons chopped fresh parsley
> freshly ground black pepper

red wine sauce

> 1 cup/250 ml/8 fl oz lamb or beef stock
> 1/4 cup/60 ml/2 fl oz red wine
> 1 tablespoon passata (tomato paste)
> 1 tablespoon Worcestershire sauce

tip from the chef

To clean a wok, wash with water (do not use detergent), then dry thoroughly. The best way to dry the wok is to place it over a low heat for a few minutes.

sweet
potato chili pork

■□□ | Cooking time: 25 minutes - Preparation time: 10 minutes

method

1. Heat oil in a wok over a medium heat, add onion, garlic, chilies and cumin seeds and stir-fry for 3 minutes or until golden.
2. Increase heat to high, add pork and stir-fry for 5 minutes or until brown. Remove pork mixture from wok and set aside.
3. Add sweet potatoes to wok and stir-fry for 5 minutes or until just tender. Return pork mixture to wok, add red kidney beans, coriander, pasta sauce and tomato paste and simmer for 10 minutes or until sauce thickens slightly. Serve immediately.

....

Serves 4

ingredients

> **2 tablespoons vegetable oil**
> **1 onion, chopped**
> **2 cloves garlic, crushed**
> **2 fresh red chilies, finely chopped**
> **1 teaspoon cumin seeds**
> **500 g/1 lb pork fillet, trimmed of all visible fat, chopped**
> **185 g/6 oz sweet potatoes, chopped**
> **440 g/14 oz canned red kidney beans, rinsed and drained**
> **2 tablespoons chopped fresh coriander**
> **1 cup/250 ml/8 fl oz bottled tomato sauce**
> **1 tablespoon tomato paste (purée)**

tip from the chef

The way in which you heat the wok and oil for stir-frying is important. Firstly, heat the dry clean wok, then add the oil by drizzling evenly down the sides of the wok. Using this method means that the wok will be coated evenly with the oil and the oil will be warm by the time it reaches the bottom.

balsamic
pork stir-fry

■■□ I Cooking time: 10 minutes - Preparation time: 10 minutes

ingredients
> **2 teaspoons olive oil**
> **2 cloves garlic, crushed**
> **500 g/1 lb pork fillet, trimmed of all visible fat, cut into 1 cm/¹/₂ in thick slices**
> **1 red pepper, chopped**
> **1 green pepper, chopped**
> **¹/₂ cup/125 ml/4 fl oz orange juice**
> **¹/₄ cup/60 ml/2 fl oz balsamic vinegar**
> **freshly ground black pepper**
> **1 bunch/125 g/4 oz rocket or watercress leaves**

method
1. Heat oil in a wok over a high heat, add garlic and stir-fry for 1 minute or until golden. Add pork and stir-fry for 3 minutes or until brown. Add red pepper, green pepper, orange juice and vinegar and stir-fry for 3 minutes or until pork is cooked. Season to taste with black pepper.
2. Divide rocket or watercress between serving plates, then top with pork mixture. Serve immediately.

....
Serves 4

tip from the chef
Balsamic vinegar is a dark grape juice vinegar. Once a delicatessen item, in recent years it has become increasingly popular and can now be purchased from supermarkets.

cajun
pork stir-fry

■■□ | Cooking time: 10 minutes - Preparation time: 10 minutes

method

1. Cut pork diagonally into thin slices (a). Place garlic, paprika, cumin, thyme, oregano and black peppercorns in a bowl and mix to combine. Add pork and toss to coat.

2. Heat oil in a wok over a high heat, add onions and stir-fry for 3 minutes or until soft. Add pork mixture and stir-fry for 3 minutes or until pork is brown (b). Add sweet corn and tomato juice to wok (c) and simmer for 3 minutes or until heated through.

....
Serves 4

ingredients

> **750 g/1¹/₂ lb pork fillet, trimmed of all visible fat**
> **1 clove garlic, crushed**
> **2 tablespoons paprika**
> **2 teaspoons ground cumin**
> **2 teaspoons dried thyme**
> **2 teaspoons dried ground oregano**
> **2 teaspoons crushed black peppercorns**
> **2 teaspoons vegetable oil**
> **2 onions, chopped**
> **440 g/14 oz canned sweet corn kernels, drained**
> **¹/₂ cup/125 ml/4 fl oz tomato juice**

tip from the chef

Meat is easier to slice if it is partially frozen. To achieve thin slices of pork, wrap in plastic food wrap, place in the freezer for 15-30 minutes or until firm, then slice using a very sharp knife.

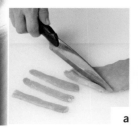
a

b

c

index